RACE FOR YOUR LIFE!

THE IDITAROD

BY KATE MIKOLEY

Gareth Stevens
PUBLISHING

HOT TOPICS

Please visit our website, www.garethstevens.com. For a free color catalog of all our high-quality books, call toll free 1-800-542-2595 or fax 1-877-542-2596.

Cataloging-in-Publication Data

Names: Mikoley, Kate.
Title: The Iditarod / Kate Mikoley.
Description: New York : Gareth Stevens Publishing, 2021. | Series: Race for your life! | Includes glossary and index.
Identifiers: ISBN 9781538259023 (pbk.) | ISBN 9781538259047 (library bound) | ISBN 9781538259030 (6 pack)
Subjects: LCSH: Iditarod (Race)–Juvenile literature. | Iditarod (Race)–History–Juvenile literature. | Sled dog racing–Alaska–Juvenile literature.
Classification: LCC SF428.7 M57 2021 | DDC 798.83–dc23

First Edition

Published in 2021 by
Gareth Stevens Publishing
111 East 14th Street, Suite 349
New York, NY 10003

Copyright © 2021 Gareth Stevens Publishing

Designer: Laura Bowen
Editor: Kate Mikoley

Photo credits: Cover, pp. 1–32 (texture) Chatham172/Shutterstock.com; Cover, p. 1 (race team) PETIT Philippe/Contributor/Paris Match Archive/Getty Images; pp. 5, 27 Troy Perano/Shutterstock.com; p. 7 Paul Souders/The Images Bank/Getty Images Plus/Getty Images; pp. 9, 23 Troutnut/Shutterstock.com; pp. 11, 25 Anchorage Daily News/Contributor/Tribune News Service/Getty Images; p. 13 Transcendental Graphics/Contributor/Archive Photos/Getty Images; p. 15 Chase Swift/Corbis/Getty Images Plus/Getty Images; p. 17 Bettmann/Contributor/Bettmann/Getty Images; pp. 19, 29 Paul A. Souders/Corbis Documentary/Getty Images Plus/Getty Images; p. 21 everydoghasastory/Shutterstock.com.

Printed in the United States of America

Some of the images in this book illustrate individuals who are models. The depictions do not imply actual situations or events.

CPSIA compliance information: Batch #CS20GS: For further information contact Gareth Stevens, New York, New York at 1-800-542-2595.

Find us on

CONTENTS

MUSHING THROUGH THE SNOW

In Alaska, **temperatures** often drop below 0°F (-18°C), and it's commonly snowy. Many people would choose to stay inside and keep warm in these conditions. But for some, it's the perfect time to race across the state. It's time for the Iditarod!

FEARLESS FACTS

The Iditarod is a dogsled race, or a race where dogs pull a **sled** across a snowy course, or trail. The person who drives the sled is called a musher.

In the world of dogsled racing, the Iditarod is the most well-known event. Every March, dozens of mushers and their dog teams gather near Anchorage, Alaska, to take part in the event that's often called "the last great race on Earth."

FEARLESS FACTS

At times, heavy winds can make it hard for mushers in the Iditarod to see. Cold conditions, darkness, and lots of hills also make for a tough, or hard, race.

THE TRAIL

The first Iditarod was held
in 1973. The race's trail is
all within the U.S. state of
Alaska. It starts in the city
of Anchorage and ends in
a city called Nome, although
the official starting point
has changed a few times.

The Last Great Race" 1049 miles

ANCHORAGE TO NOME

IDITAROD TRAIL · ALASKA ·

IDITAROD TRAIL RACE

10

START

FEARLESS FACTS

Commonly just called the Iditarod, the race's full name is the Iditarod Trail Sled Dog Race.

Teams in the Iditarod travel through snow and ice. Storms aren't uncommon. The course crosses mountains and frozen bodies of water. It's commonly around 1,000 miles (1,600 km) long, although the exact course may change a little from year to year.

FEARLESS FACTS

Early on, the race would often take 20 days.
Today, winning teams commonly finish
in fewer than 10 days.

The Iditarod's trail dates back to well before the race started. Due to heavy snowfall, it can be hard to travel by foot, or even by car, in parts of Alaska. Dogsled teams were often used for trade and to deliver, or bring, mail.

FEARLESS FACTS

In the early 1900s, gold was found in Alaska. Miners used dogsled trails to get to Iditarod, a town now **abandoned**, to get supplies for mining.

SAVING THE DAY

In 1925, many people in Nome became sick with a deadly illness. The nearest **medicine** was in Anchorage. Planes and trains couldn't reach Nome. Instead, teams of mushers and their dogs worked together to get medicine to Nome by dogsled.

FEARLESS FACTS

The lifesaving trip in 1925 **inspired** today's Iditarod. Parts of the race follow its trail, as well as old trails used for mail and trade.

PARENTS OF THE RACE

A woman named Dorothy G. Page knew a lot about Alaska's history and dogsledding. In 1973, she worked with a musher named Joe Redington Sr. to start the now-famous race. They're known as the "mother and father of the Iditarod."

JOE REDINGTON SR.

FEARLESS FACTS

Redington finished the Iditarod several times. He died in 1999, but just two years earlier he took part in his final Iditarod—at age 80!

DOG TEAMS

For years, mushers in the Iditarod could use up to 16 dogs. In 2019, the rules were changed to allow only 14 dogs per team. No new dogs can be added after the start, but some can drop out of the race.

FEARLESS FACTS

Dogs may be dropped from their team at special stopping points. This can happen if they're sick, hurt, or tired. Teams must finish with at least five of their dogs.

Many different breeds, or kinds, of dogs have taken part in the Iditarod. Today, rules say all dogs must be suitable for traveling in **Arctic** conditions. This means their bodies must be able to keep them warm and safe in the cold.

POODLE

FEARLESS FACTS

In the 1980s and 1990s, one musher in the Iditarod used poodles on his team! Today this wouldn't be allowed, since poodles aren't built for cold weather.

Dogs called Siberian huskies and Alaskan malamutes have thick coats of fur. These coats help them stay warm in cold weather. Malamutes are good at pulling heavy loads far **distances**, while huskies are naturally good at running.

FEARLESS FACTS

Today, the most common dogs in the Iditarod are Alaskan huskies. They're a mix of many breeds, including Siberian huskies and Alaskan malamutes.

Sled dogs sometimes get hurt or even die during the Iditarod. Some people are against the race because of this. To help keep dogs safe, the race has required stops for dogs to rest, eat, and get checkups from animal doctors.

FEARLESS FACTS

In 2018, the Iditarod added a rule saying that if a dog dies during the race the team will be kicked out.

THE SLED

Dogs wear a piece of gear called a harness. Lines attach the harnesses to the sled, where the musher stands and directs the dogs. Sleds often weigh around 100 pounds (45 kg). When loaded with gear and the musher, the sled weighs more than twice that much!

FEARLESS FACTS

Mushers need to dress for the cold. The
dogs must wear special booties and
often wear coats to stay warm too!

THE FAMED EVENT

The Iditarod is the most famous race in dogsledding. Dogs and mushers need to be ready to race for more than a week straight. Nearly anything can happen along the way—from falling through ice to running into animals like moose and wolves!

FEARLESS FACTS

Good mushers make sure their dogs get a lot of healthy food and rest between periods of running. Mushers need to be ready to sleep along the way too!

GEAR CHECKLIST

DOG BOOTS AND COATS

FOOD FOR DOGS AND HUMANS

WARM CLOTHING AND BLANKETS

COLD-WEATHER SLEEPING BAG

AX (TO CHOP WOOD FOR FIRES)

SNOWSHOES

TOOLS FOR COOKING

NOTEBOOK TO KEEP NOTES ON DOGS

SUPPLY KIT

FOR MORE INFORMATION

BOOKS

Gregory, Josh. *If You Were a Kid at the Iditarod.* New York, NY: Children's Press, 2018.

Heinrichs, Ann. *Alaska.* Mankato, MN: Child's World, 2018.

Jacobsmeyer, Nicki. *Surviving the Iditarod: An Interactive Extreme Sports Adventure.* North Mankato, MN: Capstone Press, 2018.

WEBSITES

Iditarod
www.alaskacenters.gov/explore/culture/dog-mushing/iditarod
Find out more about the race's trail and the dogs that take part in the event.

Iditarod
iditarod.com
Read more about the Iditarod on the race's official website.

The Sled Dog Relay that Inspired the Iditarod
www.history.com/news/the-sled-dog-relay-that-inspired-the-iditarod
Learn more about the event that started this well-known race.

GLOSSARY

abandon: to leave empty or uncared for

Arctic: to do with the North Pole and the area around it

distance: how far apart two places or things are from each other

inspire: to cause someone to want to do something

medicine: a drug taken to make a sick person well

sled: a cart with runners that moves over ice and snow

temperature: how hot or cold something is

INDEX